To My Sister

———————————————————

With Love From

———————————————————

Date

———————————————————

P9-AFE-757

SISTERS

A Gift of Memories

Barbara Briggs Morrow

Illustrations by
Denise Hilton Campbell
Jody Wheeler

new seasons™
a division of Publications International, Ltd.

Barbara Briggs Morrow is a veteran writer whose work has appeared in *Midwest Living* magazine and *Cosmopolitan*. Her previous books include *American Country Sampler, The Gift of Friendship,* and *Our Family Tree.*

Additional inspirations compiled by **Joan Loshek.**

Cover illustration by **Jody Wheeler.**

Interior illustrations by **Denise Hilton Campbell.**

Publications International, Ltd., has made every effort to locate the owners of all copyrighted material to obtain permission to use the selections that appear in this book. Any errors or omissions are unintentional; corrections, if necessary, will be made in future editions.

Copyright © 2001 Publications International, Ltd. All rights reserved. This book may not be reproduced or quoted in whole or in part by any means whatsoever without written permission from:

Louis Weber, CEO
Publications International, Ltd.
7373 North Cicero Avenue
Lincolnwood, Illinois 60712

Permission is never granted for commercial purposes.

Manufactured in China.

8 7 6 5 4 3 2 1

ISBN: 0-7853-4560-4

Contents

Childhood Memories

Because you grew up together, your sister can always see
the child you once were.

BIG SISTER, LITTLE SISTER

Where we fit in our family

_____

_____

_____

My first memories of my sister

_____

_____

_____

From the beginning, we were _____

_____

_____

_____

Being the big sister meant _____

_____

_____

On the other hand, being the little sister meant _____

_____

_____

How we felt about our roles

_____

_____

_____

Little sisters are happy that someone is blazing the trail ahead;
big sisters are comforted that someone is always close behind.

Everyone described my sister as _____

_____

_____

_____

I was known as the one who _____

_____

_____

_____

Sisters create their relationship as if it were a
mosaic. The moments they share—dreams and
secrets and games and giggles—come together one
by one. The result is an intricate and priceless work,
impossible to duplicate.

WHEN WE WERE SMALL

A typical day together

_____

_____

_____

_____

My most vivid recollection of us during those years was when _____

_____

_____

_____

_____

My favorite story about our childhood

_____

_____

_____

_____

A tale about us that I wish other family members would forget is _____

_____

_____

_____

From each other, we learned _____

_____

_____

_____

Sisters can't forget the little girls they once were,
a fact that helps keep you both young.

13

Games we loved to play

_____

_____

_____

We liked to pretend _____

_____

_____

The bedtime story we heard over and over was _____

_____

_____

Treats we always begged for

_____

_____

_____

Our best-loved toys

_____

_____

_____

Sharing becomes second nature to sisters.
It's holding back that takes effort.

SCHOOL DAYS

What we both liked most about school

_____

_____

_____

Neither of us was fond of _____

_____

_____

Playground antics

_____

_____

_____

My best subjects were _____

_____

My sister excelled in _____

_____

Times we helped each other in school

_____

_____

_____

_____

_____

_____

Graduation memories

_____

_____

_____

_____

_____

Recalling those school years, I'm proudest of _____

_____

_____

_____

Don't mind if your sister's not
overly impressed with your latest
accomplishment. She just never
expected anything less.

FAMILY MATTERS

The members of our family include _____

_____

_____

_____

Memories of our parents

_____

_____

_____

_____

_____

_____

_____

A typical day in our lives together was _____

_____

_____

In our extended family, we were closest to _____

_____

_____

Special moments in that relationship

_____

_____

_____

_____

A sister's hug wraps you for a moment
in the love and security of the home
you grew up in.

Pets we cherished

_____

_____

_____

Memories of family celebrations

_____

_____

_____

The occasion we especially looked forward to was _____

_____

_____

_____

Family traditions we loved most were _____

_____

_____

Traditions we liked least

_____

_____

Favorite family vacation stories

_____

_____

_____

_____

_____

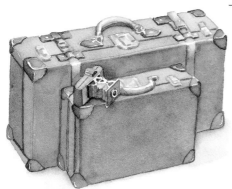

Count on your family, especially when it comes
time to count your blessings.

GIGGLES AND GRINS

As young girls, the funniest joke we shared was _____

_____

_____

_____

An embarrassing moment together

_____

_____

_____

It's hard to take yourself too seriously around your sister. She's the one who saw you with forbidden bubblegum stuck to your braces and later helped you pin up the strapless prom dress that was threatening to fall down.

Our silliest game was _____

Ways we used to tease each other

_____

_____

_____

A childhood story still guaranteed to make us giggle

_____

_____

_____

We laugh now, but a mishap that didn't seem funny at all at the time was _____

_____

_____

Blossoming Together

*The relationship between sisters is like
a perennial garden—beautiful things sprout untended,
often when you least expect it.*

DAYS TO REMEMBER

Sometimes you feel that you need two of yourself to accomplish everything.

A sister is the next best thing: an extra pair of hands; a shoulder to cry on; another foot to put down; and a leg-up on that challenge which, on your own, seemed insurmountable.

We realized that we weren't little girls anymore when _____

_____

_____

As a teenager, I couldn't have survived without her help with _____

_____

_____

And she depended on me for _____

_____

_____

A turning point in our lives at that time

_____

_____

_____

_____

If we could travel back in time to those years, the day we'd both

like to visit would be _____

_____

_____

_____

_____

SHINING STARS

Talents that we shared

_____

_____

_____

Some of the ways in which she shines are _____

_____

_____

My special gifts

_____

_____

_____

*Your sister's accomplishments can
be much more fun than your own—
everyone understands if you can't
help bragging.*

JUST FOR FUN

Memories of our favorite pastimes

_____

_____

_____

In summer, we spent our happiest hours _____

_____

_____

_____

Winter fun consisted of _____

_____

_____

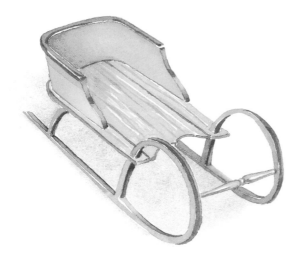

A sister is a forever friend.

<small>AMERICAN PROVERB</small>

One of our best days together was _____

_____

_____

_____

Memories of one of our most adventurous outings

_____

_____

_____

Others who often joined in on our good times included _____

_____

_____

A sister divides your cares and
     multiplies your joys.

An event we dreaded that turned out to be fun was _____

_____

_____

_____

The "fun" that almost got us into trouble

_____

_____

_____

_____

I have you fast in my fortress
And will not let you depart,
But put you down into the dungeon
In the round-tower of my heart . . .
And there I will keep you forever.

Henry Wadsworth Longfellow

Memories of big dances and other parties

_____

_____

_____

_____

Our favorite party was _____

_____

_____

_____

An activity we've enjoyed ever since is _____

_____

_____

_____

SPECIAL PEOPLE

Growing up, the person who we admired most was

_____

_____

_____

Ways in which family members influenced us

_____

_____

_____

Others who touched our lives

_____

_____

_____

_____

Special friends we shared

_____

_____

_____

Favorite stories about someone who could always make us laugh

_____

_____

_____

Lessons from teachers whom we'll never forget

_____

_____

_____

ROADS TAKEN

When she grew up, my sister always wanted to be _____

_____

My career dreams

_____

_____

_____

How those early attitudes evolved as we grew up

_____

_____

_____

For there is no friend like a sister
In calm or stormy weather;
To cheer one on the tedious way,
To fetch one if one goes astray.

CHRISTINA ROSETTI

Events that started us on our paths were _____

_____

_____

An event that in retrospect we realize was a crossroads

_____

_____

_____

The path I chose was _____

_____

_____

The route my sister selected

_____

_____

_____

Sugar and Spice

*Sisters come in perfectly matched sets and in intriguing
assortments that make you think God has quite an eye for
putting just the right mix together.*

YOU CAN TELL WE'RE SISTERS

Ways in which we look alike include _____

_____

_____

_____

We get these traits from _____

_____

_____

_____

How our similarities showed when we were children

_____

_____

_____

What others say about our similar traits

_____

_____

_____

How we're like other members of our family

_____

_____

_____

_____

An incident that illustrates this similarity was _____

_____

_____

_____

A sister is our first roommate,
our first playmate, and our
first best friend.

Positive personality traits that we share include _____

_____

_____

A less-than-positive tendency that we both have is _____

_____

_____

We both like to splurge on _____

_____

_____

_____

Your sister knows you almost as well as you know yourself. When you forget who you are, count on her to remind you.

A principle that we both believe strongly in is _____

_____

_____

_____

_____

Sometimes we almost seem to read each others' minds, like when _____

_____

_____

_____

DIFFERENT AS NIGHT AND DAY

Ways in which I am unique include _____

_____

_____

Traits that belong strictly to my sister are _____

_____

_____

Family stories about whom I take after

_____

_____

_____

Everyone says she is just like _____

_____

_____

Of course you take your sister for granted.
That's one of the beauties of the relationship.

A favorite style of hers that just isn't me is _____

_____

_____

_____

A difference between us that we tease each other about

_____

_____

_____

_____

Principles on which we agree to disagree include _____

_____

_____

_____

_____

Sometimes, we see things so differently that it's hard to believe we grew up

together. For example, _____

_____

_____

_____

_____

Closer All the Time

What is a loving sister? A single soul dwelling in two bodies.

ANONYMOUS

MEMORABLE MOMENTS

Roles we've played in each others' romances include _____

_____

_____

_____

Wedding day recollections

_____

_____

_____

_____

Births celebrated

_____

_____

_____

Work honors we've celebrated were _____

_____

_____

A behind-the-scenes story about one of her big days

_____

_____

_____

An event that brought us closer than ever was _____

_____

_____

A woman should always stand by a woman.

EURIPIDES

Reflections about an important threshold that only one of us has crossed

_____

_____

_____

Memorable birthdays

_____

_____

_____

Plans and hopes for the next big event we'll share include _____

_____

_____

_____

LAUGHING TOGETHER

We get our senses of humor from _____

_____

_____

Some of our inside jokes are _____

_____

_____

A time when laughter helped us through a tough situation

_____

_____

_____

Others might need to ask, "What's so funny?"
Chances are your sister knows and is laughing just as hard as you are.

The craziest thing we ever did together was _____

_____

_____

_____

How my sister can always make me laugh

_____

_____

_____

Something I do that's guaranteed to make her giggle is _____

_____

_____

_____

OUR ADVENTURES

Our favorite sort of expedition

_____

_____

_____

An escapade that almost plunged us into hot water was _____

_____

_____

An incident when we both were more than a little bit scared was _____

_____

_____

An everyday endeavor that turned into an adventure, thanks to my sister, was

_____

_____

_____

All about the "hair-raiser" that she blames me for

_____

_____

_____

Plans for our next adventure

_____

_____

_____

When sisters are reunited, no matter what
their age, girls are together again.

What Are Sisters For?

What are sisters for? Whatever you need
at the moment, including reminding you that
you needn't even ask the question.

SOMEONE TO LEAN ON

A ministering angel shall my sister be.

WILLIAM SHAKESPEARE

How I most often depend on my sister is _____

_____

_____

Ways in which she counts on me

_____

_____

_____

A big step that I never could have taken without her encouragement was _____

_____

_____

The important move she was able to make thanks to my help

_____

_____

_____

Little things she does for me that I appreciate in a big way

_____

_____

_____

Small ways that I help her

_____

_____

_____

The story of when it seemed we were standing together against the world

_____

_____

_____

_____

_____

Alone we can do so little; together we can do so much.

HELEN KELLER

The greatest challenge that we've faced together was _____

_____

_____

_____

Some of our small but meaningful accomplishments

_____

_____

_____

_____

SPECIAL GIFTS

The best surprise one of us gave the other

_____

_____

_____

The funniest presents we've exchanged were _____

_____

_____

_____

A present that truly was a gift from the heart was _____

_____

_____

_____

I have always loved my sister's voice. It is clear and light, a voice without seasons,
like bells over a green city or snowfall on the roots of orchids.
Her voice is a greening thing, an enemy of storm and dark and winter.

PAT CONROY, *THE PRINCE OF TIDES*

A compliment from my sister that meant a lot was _____

_____

_____

_____

Praise for my sister

_____

_____

_____

_____

THE BEST ADVICE

The most useful tip my sister ever provided was _____

_____

_____

Counsel that she received from me

_____

_____

_____

Family wisdom that we remind each other of from time to time

_____

_____

_____

_____

*There can be no situation in life in which the
conversation of my dear sister will not
administer some comfort to me.*

LADY MARY WORTLEY MONTAGUE

58

A true sister is a soulmate who listens with her heart.

ANONYMOUS

A time when she saw a situation more clearly than anyone else was _____

_____

_____

_____

My advice that I wish she would follow is _____

_____

_____

_____

The advice that she's always giving me

_____

_____

_____

_____

BETTER THAN BEST

What I enjoy most about our relationship is _____

_____

_____

_____

Ways in which we're better than even best friends

_____

_____

_____

How we maintain our connection

_____

_____

_____

You know full as well as I do the value of sisters' affections to each other;
there is nothing like it in this world.

CHARLOTTE BRONTË

Some unique aspects of the bond we share include _____

_____

_____

_____

How our bond has grown stronger over the years

_____

_____

_____

Ways I hope we can become even closer

_____

_____

_____

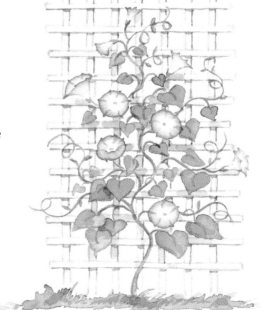

A sister is a gift of God, sent from above
to make life worthwhile here below.

ANONYMOUS

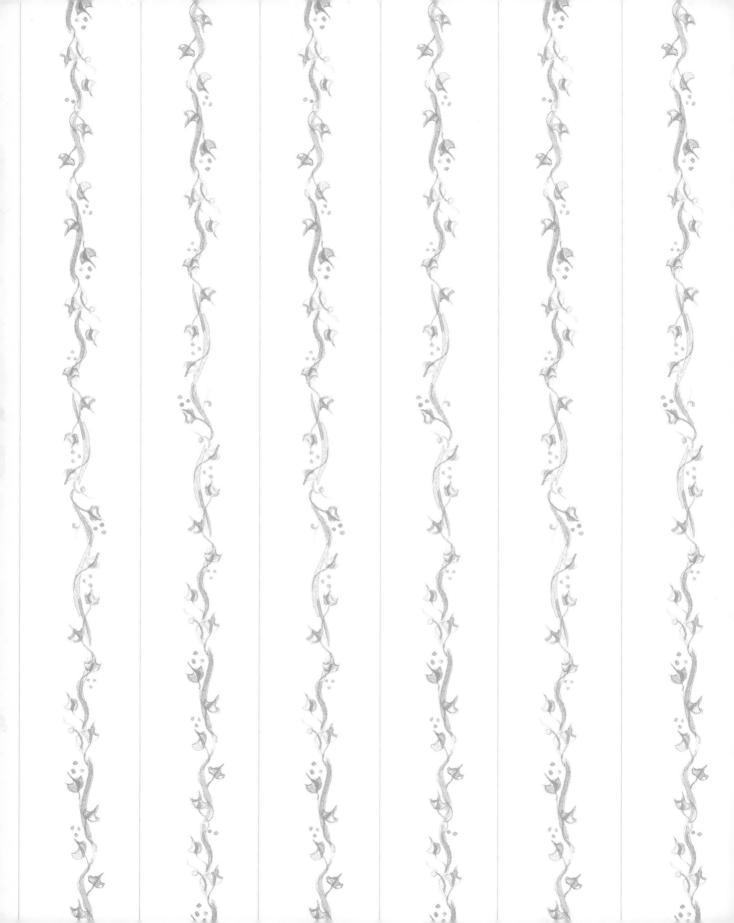